D0307428

THE
WELL
CHURCH
BOOK

Centre for
Faith and Spirituality
Loughborough University

THE
WELL
CHURCH
BOOK

A PRACTICAL GUIDE TO MISSION AUDIT
JOHN FINNEY

CPAS

Church Pastoral Aid Society
Tachbrook Park, Warwick CV34 6NG

Scripture Union
130 City Road, London EC1V 2NJ

Series editor Eddie Neale

Designed by Tony Cantale Graphics
Illustrations by Kevin Wade

This book is sponsored by the Church Pastoral Aid Society, Athena Drive, Tachbrook Park, Warwick CV34 6NG. CPAS is a mission agency which exists to strengthen churches to evangelise, teach and pastor people of all ages. It seeks through people and resources to stimulate evangelism, equip and train leaders, advise about ministry and make grants for mission and training.

© John Finney 1991

First published 1991

CIP data
Finney, John T.
    The well-church book: a practical guide to mission audit.
    1. Christianity
    I. Title
    254.6

ISBN 0 86201 549 9

All rights reserved. No part of this publication may be reproduced, stored in a retrieval system, or transmitted, in any form or by any means, electronic, mechanical, photocopying, recording or otherwise, without the prior permission of Scripture Union.

The right of John Finney to be identified as author of this work has been asserted by him in accordance with the Copyright, Designs and Patents Act 1988.

All Bible quotations, except where otherwise stated, are from the Good News Bible – Old Testament, Copyright © American Bible Society 1976; New Testament, Copyright © American Bible Society 1966, 1971, 1976.

Printed in England by Ebenezer Baylis and Son Limited, The Trinity Press, Worcester and London.

CONTENTS

PREFACE

The well–church book is intended to be the first in a series of books which will help Christians make an impact on our world – especially in urban priority areas. They are written and designed to be read by church leaders at all levels; Sunday school teachers and community workers as well as elders and church councils. And they are not just for individuals to use alone; groups of Christians can use them as handbooks with which to review their work and develop their ministry.

Books designed particularly for churches in the city are rare or non–existent. And so the series which *The well–church book* leads is a venture of faith in providing a practical resource for churches on the front line of mission.

Eddie Neale
series editor

INTRODUCTION

A lot of churches stand still because they do not know in which direction to head. This book will help them to find out (and decide).

It is a vital decision. If we do not move, we do not get anywhere, and if we go the wrong way we had better not have started.

The well–church book is about **mission audit**, which is a rather technical description for a very straightforward process. If you want to go somewhere it helps if you know where you are starting from. So this book begins by seeing how you can take the temperature of the local church, and to see it in its setting within the local community.

The second part of the book deals with finding out the **vision** that God has for your church, and the steps which need to be taken towards the vision.

The final section helps you to look at the principles which need to be borne in mind when putting your decisions into practice, and how to change things without too much hassle.

This book is meant to be used by the leadership or Church Committee to think through the way ahead. There can be nothing which is more important than finding out what is 'his good, pleasing and perfect will' (Romans 12:2).

Chapter 1

WHAT IS MISSION AUDIT ALL ABOUT?

Jesus was someone who was always asking questions. The very first time we hear of him, as a boy of twelve, he was questioning his teachers. And he kept on asking questions – often very awkward ones – because they uncovered the truth:

> **Which of these three do you think was a neighbour to the man who fell into the hands of robbers?** (Luke 10:36).

> **John's baptism – was it from heaven or from men?** (Mark 11:30).

> **'Simon son of John, do you truly love me?** (John 21:16).

Mission audit is all about asking the right questions and trying to give the right answers.

One congregration asked the obvious question, 'Who are we?' A simple questionnaire found that:

- nearly half the people who went to church were drawing their pension.
- there were a good many black people in the church but none were on the Church Committee.
- there were only six people who were getting a regular pay packet.

Our Lord knew that question and answer was one of the best ways of finding out the **truth.**

There ought to be a book called *Christians in Wonderland.* Too many live in a dream world which does not match the real life of the church round the corner from the gasworks. And that is *dangerous* – because you can't build the church of God with bricks which don't exist.

Daydreams can get in the way of what the Holy Spirit deals in: *truth – reality.*

Mission audit tries to find out the facts about the present so that we can think about the future.

Mission...audit...means:

Mission
- looking outwards as well as inwards.
- thinking about extending God's Kingdom.
- considering the community as well as the church.
- thinking about the ministry of church people at home and at work as well as in the church.

Audit
- listening (an *audio*–visual aid is what you can *hear* and see).
- trying to hear what as many people in the church and the community are really saying.
- trying to hear what God is saying.

Note: The word 'audit' is usually used of finance. But the word means much more than that – most mission audits hardly look at money.

History of the term 'mission audit'

In 1981 the Church of England asked twelve Christians from overseas to come and say what they thought about the church. They made many criticisms. In particular they said that our churches did not think carefully enough about what they were doing, and so could not decide where to go. They suggested that there should be a 'Mission Audit produced for use by all Parochial Church Councils which would enable them to examine the work of their church and community and plan for the future.' A group was set up by the Church of England Board for Mission and Unity to produce an audit. They found that it was impossible to have the same audit for every church in the land – town or country, Anglo–Catholic or evangelical, large or tiny. So they produced a booklet called *Mission Audit* to start people thinking about *how* to do an audit. **Beware** – do not be too eager to spend your £1.50 on it – it is a hard read. It might be helpful if one or two people in your church knew what it said, but it is not essential.

In 1986 The Archbishop's Commission on Urban Priority Areas reported that each UPA ought to have a 'Parish Audit' – by which they meant the same thing as a mission audit. (This makes things confusing. Both terms are used for the same thing – in this book we shall use the term *mission audit* – but if you want to call it *parish audit*....)

Appendix A of the *Faith in the City* report sets out a form for a mission audit. I think it is too lengthy and too complicated, and needs more emphasis on discovering the will of God. But it might be just right for you.

Mission audit is not:

A box of tricks   **Forecasting the future**   **Free of risk**

Nor is it the latest gimmick

It is what we have always done when we have tried to answer such questions as:

☐ 'How are we getting on?'
☐ 'Where *are* we going?'
☐ 'What are people round here really interested in?'
☐ 'I wonder how many folk in this area go to *any* church?'
☐ 'What does God want us to do?'

Mission audit just tries to be

● more methodical,
● more prayerful,
● more open,

than we have often been before.

Mission audit has two parts:

Diagnosis – what is wrong with the patient?

Treatment – what needs to happen to get the patient better?

LOOK INTO THE BIBLE

Revelation chapters 2 and 3 are very deep and challenging mission audits of seven churches. Read through them and notice:

1 each audit is addressed to the 'angel' of the church. It is not clear exactly who the angel was, but it is certainly meant someone who was in a leadership position.

Audits are especially for leaders, who have to do something about the suggestions made.

2 each audit begins with the words, 'These are the words...' – what God wanted to say to the church.

An audit is about trying to hear what God is saying.

3 each audit has the words, 'I know...'

Audits have to be based on known facts, not fantasy.

4 five out of seven audits contain criticism.

'Those whom I love I rebuke and discipline.' Few audits will only have good things to say: be prepared for the pain of audit. Truth can hurt.

5 most of the audits have more praise than criticism.

An audit should tell you what is *right* with the church, as well as what is wrong.

6 each audit reminds the church concerned of the resources of God which are available.

An audit which does not point people to God is merely an exercise in management. It will produce an earth-bound church which does not have that 'touch of heaven'.

7 each audit ends with a command to take it seriously. 'He who has ears, let him hear what the Spirit says.'

It is no use beginning an audit unless the church is prepared to study the result and act on it.

Principles of mission audit

PRINCIPLE 1
Mission audit is about people not things

Changing 'things' does not change people. For example, altering the way a church is organised may help, but does not deal with the really important matters:

- how committed people are to Christ and to the life of the church.
- what attitudes people have; to the leadership, to the community around the church and to each other.
- how prayerful people are.
- whether or not the church looks outwards.

We often try to change *things* – like church buildings, organisations etc – because it is easier.

Be careful of treating everybody in the church as though they all thought the same:

We do not all think alike, so if you catch yourself saying things like:

- ☐ 'This church thinks...'
- ☐ 'None of us want to do that...'
- ☐ 'All these white people...'
- ☐ 'All this congregation is evangelical/charismatic/catholic...'

it is not true! (All it means is that some of you think like that.)

Also, don't think that everybody in the community around thinks the same. So when you find yourself saying:

- ☐ 'Nobody around here ever thinks of God...'
- ☐ 'All they're interested in is booze and a knees up...'
- ☐ 'Can you imagine any of this lot becoming Christians...?'

watch it! Your attitude is not just mistaken – it may keep someone away from the Christ who died for them.

PRINCIPLE 2
Mission audit uses the present to think about the future

A recent survey showed that 4% of motorists on the road were lost! They knew where they wanted to go, but *did not know where they were.*

A lot of churches are lost for the same reason. They do not really know the truth about their own situation and so are unable to really pray realistically, think clearly or act sensibly.

Mission audit helps a church to find out the truth about where it is, and then think and pray about the future.

It is easy for leaders to forget that not everybody in the church knows as much as they themselves know about the church and its neighbourhood.

Mrs Smith has been a faithful member of the local Baptist church for donkey's years. She comes to the 6.30 service and goes every Tuesday afternoon to the women's fellowship. She lives on the edge of the area and goes shopping in the centre of town. If one of her neighbours asked her, she could not answer such questions as:

That is why all the Mrs Smith's in the congregation need to take part in a mission audit – so that they can share in the discovery of their own area and church.

PRINCIPLE 3
Numbers are useful but can be dangerous unless used properly

> There are three kinds
> of lies; lies, damned lies
> ...and statistics.

That is too harsh. Numbers can be important. But if we forget that numbers mean people we shall make many mistakes.

When you hear a statistic let your imagination work on it.

If you find out that there are 435 single parent families in the area, think what that means. Bringing up children all by yourself... struggling to make ends meet on the dole...rotten housing... fear of intruders.

Five more children in the Sunday school means five more children hear about the Christian faith from someone who believes it.

Don't despise numbers. They can be useful. One minister was tired of hearing how may people packed the church in the 'good old days'. A bit of research showed that the normal congregation was now higher than it had ever been. The church had been packed – but only on Mothering Sunday when they gave out the tickets for the outing to the seaside!

Numbers can tell you a lot about the people around you. Such statistics as:

- the number of unemployed people...
- the proportion of people living by themselves...
- the number of children...
- young people...
- pensioners...

can help to guide you to the right strategy for your church.

Prior Roger Schultz of Taizé says 'statistics are signs from God', because they speak about the real lives of people. And if numbers mean nothing much to you, don't bother. An audit does not depend on them.

Always remember that statistics are human beings.

PRINCIPLE 4
You need to be able to look

Teaching children to cross the road means showing them the need to

Stop...Look...Listen...Cross.

People engaged in an audit need to learn the same things.

STOP

There needs to be a time when you stop rushing about and start looking at your church. An audit gives you the chance to do that.

Some churches are like spinning tops – they feel they have to keep whirling round in case they fall over. This is sometimes called 'activism'. An activist church usually runs a series of 'events' – a mission, a summer fair, a Sunday school anniversary – and does not *stop* and *think* why they are doing those things. Or what God wants them to do.

LOOK

Not everybody is able to see what they are looking at.

> Many saw kids living in squalor under the arches of railway bridges in London. One Christian saw them as human beings in need. His name was Dr Barnardo.

LISTEN

Audit = listen.

> **It is not enough to be busy; the question is, What are we busy about?** (Thoreau)

Listen to what God is saying to the church. Prayer which expects an answer is necessary for an audit.

Hear what people are saying – not just the words, but how they are saying it and why they are saying it.

CROSS

When you have really thought about it and you know the way God wants you to go is clear – then do something about it. Just as when we are crossing the road – we need a clear *vision* before we are able to *act*.

You don't have to be clever to do an audit – but you need to be able to see what you are looking at.

PRINCIPLE 5
Make God your priority

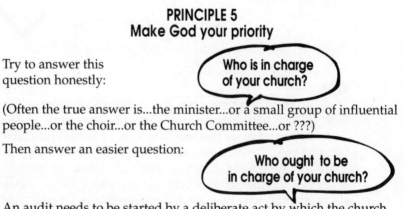

Try to answer this question honestly:

> **Who is in charge of your church?**

(Often the true answer is...the minister...or a small group of influential people...or the choir...or the Church Committee...or ???)

Then answer an easier question:

> **Who ought to be in charge of your church?**

An audit needs to be started by a deliberate act by which the church agrees to seek God's will and obey it.

St Mark's agreed to start their audit on the first Sunday in October. In preparation for this:

- all members of the congregation were given prayer cards to inform their prayers for the audit.
- quite a number of the congregation agreed to spend some time in fasting during the previous week.
- during the opening service on Sunday morning, after a time of silence, the rector led everyone in an act of dedication in which they agreed to follow God wherever he led them.

Go for growth!

What is the *aim* of mission audit? It is to help to produce a *healthy* church.

A healthy church will *grow* naturally. There is no need to keep on worrying about growth. There is no evidence that the church in the New Testament used to count the number at their services and worry if the figures were down. But they did allow God to guide them into health.

Acts 2 gives a beautiful picture of a healthy church – 'they devoted themselves to the apostles' teaching and to the fellowship, to the breaking of bread and to prayer... And the Lord added to their number daily those who were being saved.'

Just as a child will grow if she is healthy, so will a church. There is no need to keep measuring her to see if she has grown this week. The parent's job is to keep the child well fed, sheltered and happy. Growth is natural.

Symptoms of a healthy church

It has a vision of where God wants the church to go

The vision is known and welcomed by the congregation

Sensible team leadership

A good response to new ideas

Symptoms of a sick church

No vision, no direction, no focus

Members have different ideas of what ought to be happening

Uncertain leadership or a 'one man band'

'It's like flogging a dead horse'

Read on folks! ☞

Time is given for prayer and thinking and planning

Both a ceaselesss whirl of activism *and* a feeling of helplessness – 'What's the use?' – lead to little prayer, little thought and no plans for the future

The congregation and the leaders are committed to each other with realistic love and respect

Mutual suspicion and hostility – 'What's he getting up to now?' 'They are plotting something'

Tensions are out in the open and are being discussed and worked through

Tensions are:
(a) buried or
(b) allowed to fester or
(c) permitted to explode or
(d) all three!

It is aware of changes in the church and in society at large

So inward looking that they never peep outside

Good decision–making uses God's gifts wisely

Rushed, delayed or silly decisions waste people's time, money and spiritual gifts

These lead to some typical remarks.....

Good morale

Poor morale

'We need to get down to prayer about this.'

'Here he goes again....'

'I wonder if that is what God wants us to do?'

'Nobody ever told me....'

'She's got her faults but we trust her.'

'You won't catch me getting involved with that.'

'At least everybody had a chance to have their say.'

'I don't know where we're going, and I don't suppose anyone else does.'

'Isn't God exciting?'

'Boring.'

Two ideas to think about

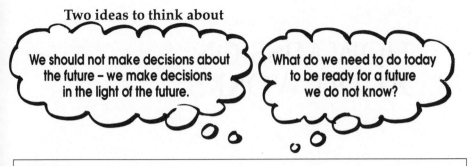

We should not make decisions about the future - we make decisions in the light of the future.

What do we need to do today to be ready for a future we do not know?

Examples

1 A small village church with a fairly good congregation (about forty out of a population of 180) asked, 'Where do we go from here?' A mission audit (which interested and involved quite a lot of people from outside the congregation) suggested various ways the church could move. After prayer, a vision was hammered out, and certain priorities for action were decided. The church moved forward with a real sense of knowing where God wanted it to go. No enormous changes happened, but morale was much higher and people began to expect God to work among them.

2 This church is on a vast, sprawling council housing estate. Looking at the congregation the church council realised that there was hardly anyone between twenty and forty. They did a mission audit which asked specifically, 'Where are the young families?' Part of the audit involved asking young families near the church why they did not come! As a result many changes took place – service times changed, a crèche was started, children's work was strengthened, a club for young mums was started etc. (Interestingly, five new young families joined the church before the audit was finished.)

3 An inner–city church had an elderly congregation which lived mainly outside the area immediately round the church. The mainly Muslim community seemed to be indifferent to the church. A new minister had come nine months before. They did a mission audit and had a real sense of God showing them several new bridges into the community – and which of the old organisations which cluttered the church ought to fold up. One new bridge in particular – a mums and toddlers group – brought many young mothers to Christ, and through them several whole families joined the church. Some of the elderly people were hurt by the death of the old organisations (though a lot were glad to be able to let go), but this feeling of resentment is now dying away. The congregation has increased in numbers – not enormously, but significantly – and there is a much greater sense of commitment to one another. Well over half the congregation now live in the immediate area of the church.

But remember: mission audit is not a recipe for instant success, it is a tool God can use if we offer it to him.

Chapter 2

HOW MISSION
AUDIT WORKS

At the heart of mission audit is a very ordinary idea. We can give it
the title

The action circle

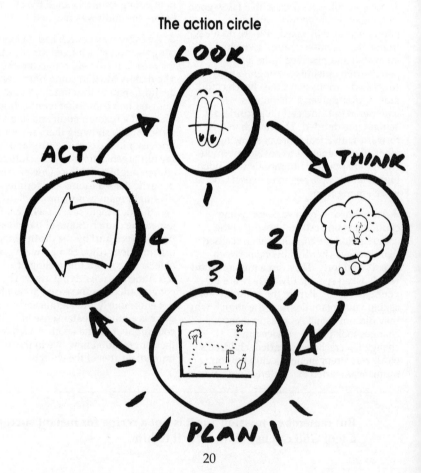

It is not as odd as it seems – we use it every day of our lives without realising it. For example:

1 I *look* in the fridge and see there is no milk.
2 I *think*: 'I shall need some milk for my cup of tea.'
3 I *plan*: 'I'll go down to the shop and get a bottle.'
4 I *act* on that plan and go and get the milk.

The action circle is used in more important things...

1 A man *looks* at his life and realises it has no real roots.
2 He *thinks* about it and wonders if there is anything the church can do to help.
3 He *plans* to go one Sunday and see if there is anything in this Christianity.
4 He *acts* upon it and turns up at an evening service.

The action circle is as natural as breathing, and nearly everything we do comes from the process. Think how it works when....

...you catch the bus,
...you open a tin of cat food,
...you say sorry for what you have done wrong,
...you clean a room.

In church we also use the action circle for very ordinary things:

1 'I can't see my song book.'
2 'The light bulb has gone.'
3 'I'll get one after the meeting.'
4 ...and then you do it.

LOOK INTO THE BIBLE

Read John 6:5–11. Where in the passage does it speak of Jesus –

    looking?   thinking?   planning?   acting?

All the examples given are of *one* person going through the 1...2...3...4 of the action circle. But it is something which a *group* of people can do. For example:

1 The Church Committee *looks* at the decoration in the church.
2 It looks dreary. They discuss it and *realise* that it spoils their worship and gives a dismal impression to newcomers.
3 They *plan* to redecorate the church. The treasurer tells them they have no money. They decide to do it themselves, and they arrange to get scaffolding and start in four weeks time.
4 They get on with it!

Notice what happens if one of these stages is left out.

If you miss out the *looking*:

you'll be like people who decide to do things without knowing what the present situation is. Their plans are not well founded, and they fail.

If you miss out the *thinking*:

you'll be like the man in the Bible who did not stop and think what the result of building his house on sand would be – a 'great crash' (Matthew 7:24–27). Thinking is hard work and we try and avoid it. After all, the man who built his house on sand finished before the man who had to hack out the foundations of his house from rock.

If you miss out the *planning*:

you will get a jumble of ideas and nothing will get done. Notice that the Church Committee in the example above had to plan the details: get the scaffolding and paint, time the start, recruit people to do the job etc. Notice also that part of planning is getting things in the right order. If the roof in the dirty church was leaking, there would be no point in thinking about the decoration until that had been put right.

If you do not *act*:

...then all your looking, thinking and planning is just so much hot air. The whole audit has been a waste of time. Some churches are always making great plans – but nothing ever happens. This means that people get frustrated, and in the end they either lose interest, or just disappear altogether.

LOOK INTO THE BIBLE

'Suppose one of you wants to build a tower. Will he not first sit down and estimate the cost to see if he has enough money to complete it? For if he lays the foundation and is not able to finish it, everyone who sees it will ridicule him, saying, "This fellow began to build and was not able to finish" (Luke 14:28–30).(Look at verses 31–33 as well.)

Jesus says in this passage:

'If you do not look ahead and plan... you are being silly.'

WHAT DOES AN AUDIT LOOK AT?

Audits are of two kinds: **general** and **limited**

1 *General* audits look at the whole work of the church in the community. Every part of the church will be covered and people will get a good idea of what makes the local community tick.

Therefore it will look at such things as:

- the healing ministry
- RE in local schools
- public worship
- why people don't go to church
- God's vision for the church
- social needs
- what tensions there are ... in the church .... in the community
- the prayer life of the congregation
- evangelistic opportunities
- where people in the community meet
- other denominations and other faiths
- why have a church hall?

2 A *limited* audit will look only at one or two parts of the life of the church or the community. The second example at the end of chapter 1 looked only at the generation gap: 'Why are there no young adults in the church?'

Other limited audits have been done in order to answer to such questions as:

> Our leadership and decision–making is in a mess: we need someone from outside to come and suggest a better pattern.

> Our church hall is falling to bits: we need to renovate it in such a way that it is of greatest use to the church and the local community. What are the needs of each of those groups?

> We have hardly any young people's work. How can we set up something which will make an impact, especially among the young Asians?

There are points for and against each kind of audit.

A general audit is good because:

+ it helps the church to get an overall picture of where it is now.

+ it helps people to think big and ask the important questions:

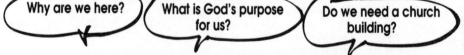

> Why are we here?

> What is God's purpose for us?

> Do we need a church building?

+ it helps people to get a vision of where God is leading them.

+ it helps to involve everyone in the congregation because it is dealing with what they are interested in. (For example, if an audit is dealing only with the question, 'What can we do to improve our morning worship?' it is not going to grab Mrs Smith who only comes in the evening.)

+ it helps church members to realise what is going on in their own church and in the local community.

+ it leads to a feeling of a job done thoroughly – the sort of feeling you get when you have finished the spring cleaning!

But
- because it looks at everything it may only look at the surface of things and not see the meaning behind them.
- it takes a fair amount of time and effort on the part of the congregation.
- it cannot be done quickly: allow about six months.
- it needs care in setting it up so that people do not get confused by so many facts and ideas.
- it can produce a great mass of ideas which need a lot of sorting out. (One audit ended with 189 different suggestions of what ought to be done!)

A limited audit is good because:
+ it can look more deeply at the area it is covering and is therefore more thorough.
+ it is less of a threat to people (and therefore may be more easily accepted in a UPA area).
+ it takes less time and trouble. A general audit usually means that a church can undertake nothing much else while it is going on.
+ it can help a congregation which knows where God is leading it really to understand the meaning of that vision.
+ it tends to produce quite detailed plans for action.

But
- it takes for granted that the area it is going to look at is the right one. It might be that God wants the church to look in a totally different direction. If a limited audit is done the church needs to be sure of the direction it ought to go in.
- it can be chosen by a church because it seems safer than a general audit, which could uncover all sorts of uncomfortable things!
- it tends not to tackle the really big questions, such as 'Why do we have a church?'
- it is difficult to keep looking at only the area which has been chosen – though this can be an advantage as well!
- it may not interest all the congregation.

Normally...

**'If you want to know where God is leading you
   – have a *general* audit.'**

**'But if you already know where God is leading
   – have a *limited* audit.'**

Note one: An important exception to this rule is: 'Where a church is particularly weak it is better to have a limited audit which it can tackle successfully than a general audit which it can't.'

Note two: Remember that an audit can be like a ball of string – pull one bit and you get the lot. A limited audit can be a way of looking at much more than you intended. Notice how the third example in chapter 1 brought in such things as times of services, type of worship etc, which they had not intended to cover when they began the audit. (This may be particularly important in UPA churches.)

Note three: Nearly all the material published for audits is for general audits. Don't despair – read on!

OUCH!

An audit which does not cause some pain is not worth having. To spend a lot of time in order to discover that the church is wonderful is not likely to be helpful – or true!

An audit is rather like going to the dentist – you are fairly sure that you are going to get hurt sometime, but you are not quite sure when.

It is sensible to know beforehand the areas which are likely to be sore:

1 'Pet ideas'

Every church does things in a certain way – usually the way the minister wants it! An audit will ask, 'Why do you do it like that?' – or even, 'Why do you do that at all?'

We don't like this sort of question, and wriggle.

2 Leadership style

Any general audit is going to look at the way in which the church makes decisions and acts on them. There are various comments which give away the style of the leader:

- ☐ 'He tells us what we need to do.'
- ☐ 'We seem to talk and talk and never come to any conclusion.'
- ☐ 'I don't know who makes the decisions.'
- ☐ 'We just seem to drift along.'
- ☐ 'We make decisions but nothing ever seems to change.'

Good leaders will welcome an audit because it helps them to think about and improve the way they lead.

Leonard Cheshire VC, founder of the Cheshire Homes, describes what it was like to give up control of them: 'If it is an undertaking that we ourselves have brought into being...it may prove almost impossible to force ourselves to hand over the reins because we tend to look upon our own creation as we would upon our own child...but the act of delegation proved to be a liberating experience.'

---

3 Growth

Nearly everybody says, 'I want my church to grow.' But not everyone likes the results of growing. A church which is growing in numbers becomes less personal, less cosy, less friendly. One regular churchgoer said, 'I went to church this morning and it seemed to be full of strangers.'

The leaders of a growing church have more people to care for and so have less time for each person. (And usually they spend too much time with a very few people who demand a lot of attention.)

An audit can help people to take the wide view, and welcome growth for the sake of the Kingdom of God rather than grumble about its effect on themselves.

An audit can set up a plan for growth and suggest ways in which the 'growing pains' can be coped with.

4 'Boils'

The quarrel between two leaders in the church at Philippi was poisoning the whole body of Christ. It was a 'boil' which had to be dealt with. So Paul says, 'I plead with Euodia and I plead with Syntyche to agree with each other in the Lord' (Philippians 4:2).

Most churches have 'boils'. Besides people who do not get on with each other they can be:

Wrong people in the right place...
- a Sunday school teacher who is not good with children.
- a house group leader who throws his weight around.
- an organist who cannot help to lead worship.

Right people in the wrong place
These are people with gifts which ought to be used properly in other areas: eg an evangelist on the Fabric Committee. If they are not moved they become discontented because they are not allowed the freedom to be themselves.

People who have been too long in one place
I was once asked to give a presentation to a churchwarden in a village church who had been in the job for forty–four years. Everyone had wanted him to go but they had not had the courage to vote him out. One older member of the congregation told me after the ceremony, 'He used to be so good when he first started, but...'

To help with this common problem...
either of these suggestions may be some help.

'*Terms of office*' If people know before they begin that they will serve for only a certain length of time, it means they can retire gracefully at the end of their 'term of office'.

One Anglican diocese suggests:

- Churchwardens – six years
- Treasurer – eight years
- PCC members – three years

– with a year's gap before they can be re–elected.

'*Career structure*' If people are to move on from being officers in the church there needs to be somewhere for them to go!

It should be suggested that they could have another office within the local church, or outside

- in the denomination,
- the community, or
- a struggling church nearby.

5 How others see us

Part of a proper audit will find out what people outside the church think of it. It can be like a bath in cold water:

Not all comments should be taken too seriously – a lot of people like to sound off about the church. But if a criticism is common, it needs to be taken to heart because it will hold back the church's evangelism.

Not all comments will pull you down. Here are some statements I have heard (from non–churchgoers) about churches where I have been doing audits:

6 'Ruffled feathers'

An audit is bound to be about change. Some people find any sort of change very difficult to cope with. It is possible to bring in changes sensibly and smoothly, but some people are going to be upset for a time. (This is such an important subject that the whole of chapter 8 has been given to it.)

7 Groups past their 'sell–by' date

One of the hardest things in any church is to say, 'This organisation ought to finish,' or, 'That group ought to change.' It may be a men's fellowship, or a prayer group, or a choir. (If you find this difficult you are not alone. Every group which depends on people giving their time freely finds 'redundancy' hard. The Scouts, the St John's Ambulance Brigade and many others have found this one of the trickiest things to handle.)

If an audit suggests that an organisation should change there may be:

- anger: 'This has been part of my life...'
- relief: 'Thank goodness, we have been propping it up for years.'
- acceptance: 'Well, if that is how you want it...'

In a general audit each organisation will need to be looked at and the possibility of change should be made clear to them. People in even the best of organisations find it good to look at what they are doing and why.

All this talk of pain makes it seem that an audit is like being put on the rack. This is not true. Most audits have very little discomfort and a great deal of joy and Christian commitment. All the same, it has been sensible for us to look at the areas where there might be difficulties.

DO WE NEED HELP?

Many audits are D-I-Y. The congregation looks at itself – often using a published pattern of questions – and makes up its own mind.

Other churches invite one or more outsiders to come and help with the audit. It has to be said straightaway that these people do not come in to do the audit for you, but to do it with you. In other words they give advice and encouragement, but they do not find out the facts and do the thinking themselves. They are fellow Christians from another church who have come to give you a hand.

These 'outsiders' can be called 'auditors', 'observers', 'friends' etc, etc. We will call them 'Advisers' in this book – but choose a name you feel comfortable with. It doesn't matter much provided you don't call them something harsh, like 'inspectors' or 'investigators'!

Needless to say there are both good and bad points in both ways of doing an audit, and it is sensible to see which is right for you. The areas which you will need to consider are:

1 Control
In D–I–Y audits you are in control of the whole thing. You don't have to consider anybody else. On the other hand, Advisers can suggest ways an audit can be done better.

2 Difficult matters
Outsiders can say things which are too difficult for anyone in the church to say. For example, it may be better for Advisers – rather than anyone in the church – to say that Mr Bigmouth has been in office too long.

3 Pain
It is good to have a 'lightning conductor' around who can deflect anger. It is easier for people to say, 'It was those people from outside who suggested it', than to admit that your own friends did so.

4 Weight
Some people pay more attention to what is said by people they know. However most give more weight to what 'experts' from outside say. (Remember that people from outside are seen as 'experts', even if they have never done an audit before in their life.)

5 Confidentiality

Clearly any Adviser needs to know what is happening in the church, and some in the congregation may be uneasy about it. On the other hand such people may need to be asked, 'What have you got to hide from the rest of the church of Christ?' It must be made clear to any Advisers at the start that the church expects them to keep anything they learn to themselves.

6 Resources

Outsiders can suggest ways of getting round problems, or give ideas that the church can try.

7 Freedom

Some churches find it difficult to tell people from outside about themselves. People in the downtown areas get fed up with 'inspectors' from the DSS, school attendance officers and social workers. They may not like the idea of having their church looked at by people from outside.

   If this feeling is around then it is important that the Advisers meet the congregation before the audit is arranged. Then they will be seen as Christian friends who have come to help the church rather than inspectors sent in by the circuit, the diocese or the presbytery.

8 The obvious

You walk across the carpet in your room so often that you have stopped noticing the big stain near the door. The same can happen in churches. Often an Adviser can point out things which are obvious. You can see them as well – when you stop and look.

On the whole I think most churches would be best to have Advisers to help them. But there are exceptions.

   If you decide to have Advisers then there are other questions:

Who should we have to help us?

Quite a number of denominations have recently set up local teams who are able to help in this work. They have had some training, and have some experience. It makes it seem 'official' to have someone like this. This is helpful in some churches – less so in others!

It is possible for the leaders to get a friend from another church to come and help. Be careful! If your church sees the friend as someone who has been invited in by the minister or by a group in the church to fire their bullets for them he or she may not be trusted. As a result anything which is said will not be accepted.

How many should we have?

Many churches have one Adviser to help. My own experience is that two is better: they can compare notes, cover more ground, have different ideas. It is especially helpful if one of them is a minister and the other a layperson, and one is a woman and the other is a man. It is surprising how differently people see things!

Some churches have had five or six or even more. This may be useful in very large churches where there are many different parts of the work and the Advisers can share it between themselves. St Michael–le–Belfrey in York had this kind of audit.

Whether you decide to have Advisers to help or go it alone, you will need to make a start.

Chapter 3

SETTING UP

A mission audit needs to involve as many people as possible.

This chapter shows a way in which this can be done. It has worked in a large number of churches, but find out what is right for you.

A church is made up of different groups of people:

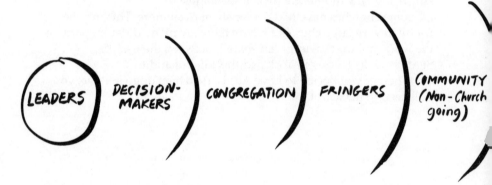

If you are doing a mission audit:

- The **leaders** must be convinced that this is God's will for the church – they are usually the minister and any others who have overall responsibility for the church.
- The **decision–makers** must give it their full support – usually they are the members of a Church Meeting, PCC, Elders Meeting etc. To keep it simple I have called it the 'Church Committee'.
- The **congregation** must be told in such a way that they come to welcome it.
- The **fringers** and the non–churchgoing **community** need to be drawn in at some stage.

The way it happens is often like this:

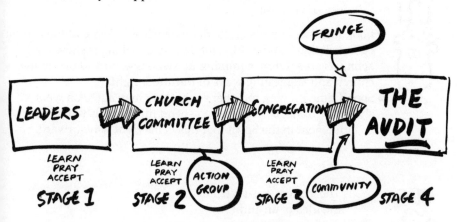

STAGE 1
The leaders

The leaders can *learn*
about mission audit.

- Read books about audit. (At this stage read about doing an audit, rather than just read a published method of doing an audit. You need to know what an audit can and can't do before deciding on the way in which you are going to do it.) This book is meant to help at this stage.
- Hear what others have done. Invite a church which has done an audit to send a few people over to talk about it. Better still, go and visit them. (But don't just copy the way they did their audit: their church is different from yours.)
- Talk with someone who has been an Adviser and helped other churches to do audits.
- Discuss it thoroughly and think how it could happen in your church.

The leaders must *pray*
about an audit.

- Look together at parts of the Bible which show an audit in action: eg Revelation 2 and 3. 1 Corinthians and Galatians show Paul acting as an Adviser, summing up what is good and bad in the church and suggesting ways of putting it right.
- Spend time praying together so that you may agree on what should be done. Be prepared to spend time on this until there is an agreement in the Spirit that this is the right way forward.

The leaders must *accept*
the idea of an audit.

- You make a clear decision to go forward to stage 2.
- You agree on what you are going to suggest to the Church Committee about:
  (a) whether to have a general or limited audit.
  (b) if it is to be a limited audit, what areas you should look at.
  (c) whether to have the help of an Adviser.
  (d) whether or not to have an Action Group.
     (See below for what an Action Group is.)
  (e) whether to do it alone or with other churches.

Involving other churches has plus points (+ wider viewpoint, + help from others) and minus points (– not all may be equally enthusiastic, – a joint report may mean nobody acts on it).

Note: Do not rush your decision. *Never* learn...pray...accept all at one meeting. Be prepared to take up to several weeks – you will get a better decision in the long run.

STAGE2
The Church Committee

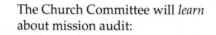

The Church Committee will *learn*
about mission audit:

- by hearing others. People learn best from people. You can use:
 (a) the leaders, who put forward what they have agreed.
 (b) one or two people from another church to talk about
  their audit.
 (c) someone from outside your church who knows about
  mission audit.

Note: I have found in practice that (b) and (c) are much more
satisfactory. If the leaders talk about the idea there will always be
those who are 'agin the government.'

- by reading. Be careful not to give people too much to read. (One
 church gave every member of its Church Committee a copy of
 the booklet *Mission Audit* to read. It killed the idea stone dead!)
- by talking it through thoroughly. Allow people to bring up
 problems and to say what they are really feeling. Give plenty
 of time so that no one feels they have not had a chance to have
 their say.

Note: You may find that one or two members of the committee have
suffered under a 'management consultancy' at work. Explain that an
audit is very different – it is the church looking at itself, not being
shredded by someone from outside.

The Church Committee must *pray*
about the audit:

- by spending time in prayer at the meetings.
- by allowing time for members to pray at home.
- by mentioning the subject in church and prayer groups.

The Church Committee *accepts*
the idea of having an audit.
Once the Committee has agreed, there are important questions which
have to be decided on:

Puddlecombe Church Committee

Agenda:

1   Is it to be a general or a limited audit?

2   If it is to be a limited audit, what areas of church and
community are to be looked at?
(If the Committee looks as though it is going for a
limited audit because it seems safer, stress that this is a
mission audit.)

3   Are Advisers going to be invited to help? If so who are
they to be?

4   Are all the members of the Committee personally
prepared to make it work – by turning up at meetings,
helping to explain it to the congregation etc?

5   Who is going to get it going?

Usually an Action Group of about six people is set up.
These might be:

(a) the minister
(b) one or two of the 'heavyweights' in the church –
steward, churchwarden etc.
(c) one or two who are not on the Church Committee.

Have a good mix of sex, colour and age. They should not
be all of the same outlook.

Note one: **Time** – do not rush this. Read chapter 8 on how to help people to accept change.

Note two: **Opposition** – it is not wise to go on with the idea of an audit if there are a fair number of people against it. Remember, the Church Committee not only sets the audit up. It also makes sure something happens afterwards. So if there are a fair number of people who do not like the idea in the first place there is the danger that any plans which come out of it will not be acted upon by the Committee. I would not be happy to do an audit where there was a 60/40 split.

STAGE 3
Telling the congregation

Use every possible way of getting the congregation to learn about, pray about and accept the idea of mission audit.

1 Explain what it is all about – at church services, fellowship meetings, etc. (Don't just give out a notice – nobody remembers them.) It is a new idea to nearly everyone, so it will need repeating over and over again in every way possible.
2 Talk to people one to one if you feel they are unhappy about it.
3 Bring someone in from outside to talk about the idea of mission audit. Again, a team from a church, or someone who knows something about it will do this best.
4 Write about it in the church newsletter. Even send a special letter to each member of the congregation.
5 If you are doing it with other churches there will need to be some way in which the congregations can meet each other. A big meeting or service will help. If this is impossible then the Church Committees should get to know each other.

Note one: It is not only in inner–city areas that people learn best through a story. Someone telling what happened in another church is better than a lot of explanation.

Note two: Once again, don't rush it. It takes several weeks for an idea to travel round a congregation and sink in. Get people's interest by doing something out of the usual.

Two churches...

One church put up a large street map of the area at the back of the church. As people left the services they were given coloured pins to stick in the place where they lived. It got their attention and gave some useful answers to important questions – eg:

- Do the church leaders live near the church?
- Are there 'clusters' of people who might become house groups?
- Do the numbers of churchgoers drop off with distance from the church

building? If so, a new congregation might be 'planted' in a school or community building in those areas.

Another church (very conservative in outlook!) turned the time usually given to the sermon into a discussion. The congregation broke into groups to talk about, 'What would you like this church to be like in the year 2000?' The time was led by an Adviser – I'm not sure the minister would have got away with it! It worked well and everybody wanted to go deeper into the question.

STAGE 4
The fringe and the wider community

If the audit is to be a *mission* audit it is important that people outside the church should be involved. Here are some ways I have found that this has been done:

1 One church invited each of the four other denominations in the area to send two 'observers' to take part in the audit. They were glad to be asked. The observers played a big part and went back home asking, 'When are *we* going to have an audit?'

2 Another church asked the headteachers of the local schools to a small meeting with the Action Group and Advisers to find out (a) what they thought of the church and (b) what the church could do to help them. It was very useful. The schools felt more part of the community and the church got an open door for work in the schools.

3 Before the audit began a church invited some social workers to come and talk of the social pressures they had found in the area. It led on to a regular meeting between the churches and the social workers.

4 Several churches have done 'spot' surveys of their neighbourhood using a questionnaire. They asked people's views on the Christian faith, the community and the local church. The results made excellent material for the audit. (A 'spot' survey is less hard work than a complete one: eg, you visit the 7th and 37th house in every street.)

5 Churches have found that 'fringe' churchgoers need to be personally invited to take part. Many will come if they see that what they say will be taken notice of. Usually churches find that they are no longer fringers by the time the audit is finished.

Use your imagination to see what would be possible in your area!

...Meanwhile

The Action Group has sprung into life.

The group will need to meet fairly soon after the Church Committee has agreed to have an audit. If Advisers are being invited to help they also will need to be there. There is a lot to decide and it can take some time.

The menu for the meeting will look something like this:

Puddlecombe Church Action Group

Agenda:

1 Prayer (and welcome to Advisers).
2 Recap on what mission audit is all about.
3 What are we auditing?
4 What method of audit shall we use?
5 Who needs to be involved?

- Who is going to ask them?
- Do they need training?
- If so, when and by whom?

6 How can we tell the congregation and others about the audit?
7 (If you are using Advisers)

- At what points are the Advisers going to be involved?
- Do they produce a summing–up at the end?
- Who pays their expenses?

8 (If you are not using Advisers)

Who is going to write the summing–up?

9 Date of next meeting.
10 Prayer.

This such an important meeting it is sensible to look more closely at each item on the menu.

Item 1: Prayer

Prayer must not just be a formal nod towards God. Everyone needs to give themselves to the Lord for the task.

Item 2: Recap

Not everyone will have been at the Church Committee meeting – and some who were there will have forgotten a lot of what was said. Go through the reasons for the audit as well as describing the practical things which have to be done.

Item 3: Scope

Check again that everyone is clear what is the scope of the audit. This is particularly important if it is to be a limited audit.

Item 4: Method?

This is probably the most important decision of the meeting. At the end of this chapter there are examples of the sorts of audit which have been used.

General audits tend to come in two flavours:

(a) a fairly detailed list of questions on the different areas of the life of the church and the community. This can be a good many pages long.

(b) a few general questions which introduce discussion on the various areas of church and community. This kind of audit is probably no longer than a single sheet of paper.

(You will find that nearly all audits are based on the action circle we looked at in chapter 2.)

It can be said that both kinds need care. The first will give a lot of ideas, but people can become bogged down in the mass of paper. The second needs leaders who can make people think carefully about what their bright ideas really mean. I have seen both kinds used in inner–city areas and there was no great difference in the result. However in one church where there were a fair number of people who could not read well the first method asked too much of them.

Possibly more important is the *way* in which the audit is done. This time there are three flavours:

(a) As many as possible of the congregation are asked to join a group. These groups meet once a week for five or six weeks.
(b) Two or three church meetings are held, at which the questions of the audit are discussed. Usually the meeting splits into small groups for part of the time. These then report on what they have talked about.
(c) A church weekend or a couple of Saturdays are given to talking about the audit.

You will find that almost all the audits which are published assume that you are going to use method (a). But not all churches take kindly to groups, and find (b) or (c) are better. Leadership is vital. If you have enough group leaders you can trust, you will probably find that method (a) will suit best. But if you are short of good leaders (b) or (c) are easier. If you are using Advisers they will probably lead (b) or (c) themselves. (One church neatly got over the difficulty about group leaders by asking another church to lend them twelve. It worked very well, and the leaders could not be accused of plugging their own line.)

This is a big decision. Take time on it. You will find that Advisers can help you on this if you have them. Some Advisers will even write an audit specially for you. This is almost essential if you are having a limited audit because there is virtually no published material.

Item 5: Who?
The answer to this depends on what you have already decided. If you are going to use groups you will need to pick group leaders and train them. It is particularly important to have a good 'scribe' in each group who can record what is said, because this will be the basis for the final summing-up. (If there is no one who writes well you can use a tape recorder, but it is a big job for someone to listen to it all and sort out what needs to be put down.)

Details need to be sorted out at the meeting. If time is short one or two people can be asked to do it later.

● If you already have groups meeting regularly it is often best not to keep them intact, but break them up during the audit. Their members know how groups work, and if this is spread around it can help others. (They can also become mini-pressure groups!)

● Most ministers can kill a group dead in two minutes! However nice they are, people expect them to do the speaking. Also the group may want to discuss the leadership of the church, which is difficult with the minister present.

Item 6

Read through what was said earlier about stages 3 and 4. Some Action Groups have found it useful to have a 'brainstorm' to get people thinking freely and producing good ideas – just chuck out ideas as they come to you, however silly they may seem, and then see if there is gold among them.

Item 7

If you are using Advisers...

Work out with them when they can come and visit your church in action. If I am an Adviser, I usually find that it is good to be at:

● the launch of the audit – most churches have a special Sunday.
● a meeting of the Church Committee (not to say anything – just to look and see).
● an ordinary Sunday, when I can sit in the congregation and worship with them.
● a meeting with the minister (sometimes with the 'heavyweights' too) to talk over things as he or she sees them.
● any social events when I and my fellow-Adviser have a chance to meet as many people as possible.

Dates need to go in diaries and firm arrangements need to be made.

Travelling expenses need to be met. Advisers should not be out of pocket because they are there helping you. (If this is a real problem, some denominations have funds which could help.)

It is no use finishing the audit and then saying, 'Oh dear, we ought to produce a summing-up.' It needs thinking about as early in the audit as this. It deserves a section to itself.

The summing-up

You will need a summing-up at the end of the audit. It can set down what has been decided and be a guide for the future. (Sometimes this is called a 'report' – but we may much not like the word because it reminds us of school. If you would rather use it, by all means do so.)

There is no need to be frightened by the idea of this. I have seen some summings-up which were over a hundred pages long – but most of them are two or three pages. Usually the shortest are the best.

I have written quite a number of these. If I can set down some of my own experience...

1 There is no need to describe the past of the church in any detail. Henry Ford said, 'History is bunk'. He might also have said, 'History is dangerous' – because one person will not see what has happened in a church in the same way as another. An audit is more interested in the future of a church than its past. Arguments about what happened in the past are seldom fruitful.

2 The most important part of a summing-up is what we would like to see happen as a result of the audit – the 'recommendations'. These are what everybody will look at most closely. So they need to be set out clearly in a way that people can understand.

3 A summing-up is much more easily accepted by a church if it has been chewed over by a group of people in the church itself before it is in its final form. If it is seen as just the work of one person in the church or of a couple of Advisers from outside, it is easy to rubbish it: 'They can't really understand us.' But if it is talked through with people in the church and altered in the light of what they say it is far more likely to be taken seriously. When I am acting as an Adviser we write a first draft of the summing-up and then talk it through with the Action Group. Afterwards we change it a lot because of what they have said. It takes longer but makes a much better job in the end.

4 Groups, or the Church Meetings, will have written down their findings. Quote their words whenever possible.

5 Avoid words which are too generalised and too easily quoted. One summing-up had the phrase, 'This church is more interested in hogroasts than holiness': it laid itself open to the charge, 'Does that mean all of us?'

Setting an audit up involves asking a lot of questions. Some of them we've had to skim over in this chapter: but we'll look at them later on. 'What kind of audit shall we use?' is one of those questions. Chapter 4 looks at different kinds of audit, how to choose one, and how to get things going!

Chapter 4

KINDS OF AUDIT

What's on the market?

If you look at any audit you will find that it makes use of the action circle (see chapter 2). They will include a time for:

LOOKING   THINKING   PLANNING   ACTING

Note: All published audits are 'general'. Because limited audits are usually just for one church they have to be produced specially. (The difference between 'general' and 'limited' audits is given on pages 23 and 24.) It is not too difficult to make up your own D-I-Y limited audit by picking the right bits out of general audits.

You will find that published audits will tend to be either:

1 Like Scotland Yard

This audit is a detailed investigation of all the things which the church and the community do. From this a picture of everything emerges. From this the people doing the audit can find what the vision is.

2 Like poetry

This audit helps you to begin to dream dreams. You then have to work out what you have to *do* in order to make the dream become real.

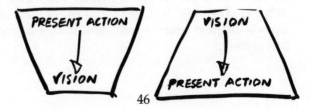

You can often tell the difference between the two types of audit simply by length. Usually type 1 is much longer – type 2 may be only a page of paper with five or six questions.

Each has both good and bad points.

Type 1

+ forces people to look at the real situation.
+ can be easier for leaders who are not very experienced.
+ means that areas of work in the church and the community are not left out.
+ gives the sense of a thorough job when it is finished.

But...

– it does not work so well if you are not in groups but in a larger meeting (ie methods (b) or (c) on page 43).
– it can look rather frightening when it is first looked at.
– it is possible to get bogged down in the details and fail to get a vision.
– it can be too clear cut and stop people dreaming their dreams and telling their stories.

Type 2

+ means people lift their eyes above the present because it starts with their dreams.
+ is simple to understand and cheap to produce.
+ is usually best where churches decide to meet all together rather than in groups (ie methods (b) or (c) on page 43).
+ allows more room for imagination and story telling.

But...

– dreams have to be earthed – and there is a danger of never getting down to practical affairs (though the 'stats sheet' (see below) will help to prevent this).
– it needs good leadership.
– it means you can waste time discussing things which do not matter.
– it can make people uneasy at the end because they say, 'Have we left anything out?'

What is available

Nearly all commercially published audits are type 1. Those produced by dioceses and other church bodies can be either type 1 or 2.

Among audits produced particularly for inner–city areas are:

Parish audit – switching the style, Evangelical Urban Training Project, PO Box 83, Liverpool L69 8AN

An audit for the local church , Church House Publishing, Great Smith Street, London SW1P 3NZ

Most denominations have people who can put you in touch with what is currently on the market – diocesan missioners, directors of evangelism, social responsibility officers, urban officers etc.

Addresses and telephone numbers of organisations can be found in the *UK Christian Handbook* (MARC).

Note one: Some of the larger audits have sections which can be done separately. For example, the excellent *Mission Pursuit*, published by the United Reformed Church, covers many different subjects, and is intended to be a 'pick 'n' mix' counter from which you can choose what is right for you.

Note two: It is not always necessary for you to buy a copy of the audit for everyone taking part. Some need just a copy for each leader. Several audits are kind enough to invite you to photocopy the material (eg *An audit for the local church,* produced by the Anglican Board for Mission and Unity).

Note three: Be prepared to alter the material in order to suit the people in your church. The motto of the Round Table is a good one: 'Adopt, adapt and improve.'

'Stats sheet'

Whichever kind of audit you are doing you will find it very useful to prepare a 'stats sheet' showing the main statistics which the people doing the audit need to know.

Very few people know all the facts about the church and the neighbourhood. It is important that they find out. Otherwise they will argue fruitlessly about details that nobody is sure of.

One of these sheets should be given to each person taking part in the audit. Don't give it only to the leaders – it is never comfortable feeling that someone in the group has more information than you do.

Do not be frightened about preparing a 'stats sheet'. Most of the facts can be found out with a few phone calls or letters.

Facts about the social life of the community can often be found from surveys which have been carried out by Social Services, or by Universities or Further Education Colleges. Often public libraries can be useful. Many denominations have someone called a social responsibility officer or similar. They are usually very helpful in telling you where information can be found.

A specimen 'stats sheet' is given in the Appendix at the end of the book. You could decide to gather lots more information, but don't overdo it!

Map

A street map of the area is extremely useful since few people know their locality well.

Half an hour can be usefully spent putting on the map:

- the main meeting places,
- the schools,
- hospitals, prisons etc,
- churches and places of non–Christian worship.

(This is a good way of breaking the ice at the first meeting.)

Choosing the right audit

There are many possible audits. There are several different ways of tackling them. Getting the one which is right for your church is important. It needs *prayer* and *care* to find what is best for you.

Pray: This is God's work. Ask for his guidance.

Think 1: What sort of people are in your church?
Does the audit you are looking at:

- use words which are not likely to be understood?
- demand more reading that most can cope with?
- ask people to do a lot of thinking on their own?
- need more knowledge of the Bible than many have?
- ask people to write things down? Is this difficult for some?
- allow a group to fall behind schedule? (People can feel failures if they fall behind a tight programme.)

Think 2: What sort of leaders have you got?

Does the audit:

- give them enough help to lead properly?
- give too much direction (and so limit what the leaders can do)?
- fail to grab people's interest? A bored group is much harder to lead.
- use visual aids which your leaders could manage?

Think 3: How is the audit presented?

Does it:

- seem dull or interesting?
- use friendly language? (Some audits sound like touchy teachers – 'Do this'... 'Do that').
- have visual aids which are real helps to teaching and not just gimmicks?
- encourage people to learn from each other and not just from the 'book'?
- suggest that people tell stories as well as talk about ideas?
- give much too much material for each session? (A little too much is often helpful – it makes a group or meeting get on with it – but too much overwhelms people.)
- allow space for those doing the audit to dream their own dreams – or are they forced in a certain direction?
- use jargon?

Think 4: What is the content of the audit?

Does it:

- try to link the church with the community? (Some audits tend to think only of the church.)
- explain basic ideas carefully?
- get the imagination going as well as the mind? Some audits seem as visionary as the instructions for a washing machine.
- waste time on useless exercises?
- have a lot of questionnaires? (These can be useful, but too many are difficult to assess and draw together at the end of the audit.)
- talk about God and his will?

It is important to go through these questions carefully. If you are a local leader you can often improve on a printed course and make it fit your own situation.

An audit should help the church to think and dream:
– it should not do its thinking and dreaming for it.

Getting it launched

Presentation of the audit

An audit should look good. It should be:

- *readable* Smudged type that has been reduced too much is hard to read and uninviting. Use plenty of white space round the writing. Use diagrams and pictures where possible.
- *well–produced* If you fasten some sheets of paper together with a paper–clip it looks tatty and soon comes to bits. Put a plastic cover with a coloured spine round the same papers and it looks much neater and more professional.
- *localised* If possible put a local name on it. Even a cover with the name of the church and the date on it can work wonders. The 'stats sheet' will help in this.

An audit which is poorly presented gives the impression that it is not important.

Training group leaders (for method a)

If the group method of doing an audit is being followed there should be at least one training session with the group leaders. If possible each group should have at least two leaders: they can help each other, share the burden and give wiser leadership.

The scribes, who write down the main findings of the group, should also be invited.

If you are using Advisers they could well be asked to take the session.

It will be used to:

(a) introduce people to the written audit,
(b) enthuse them with what is being done and what might come out of it,
(c) tell the leaders and the scribes what to do,
(d) hand out materials for visual aids etc,
(e) calm the fears of everybody concerned!

Probably about ten days before the launch of the audit is about the right time for this meeting.

The meeting should be *well planned* and have plenty of time for *prayer*.

- If it is badly prepared it gives the hint to the leaders that they also can be sloppy in running their sessions.
- If there is little prayer it suggests that God does not come into it.

The scribes should be told how important their work is.

- What they write will be the only way in which the group discussion will get reported to those making the summing–up.
- By asking for clarification on points which are being discussed they will help the group leader(s).
- They do not need to report every discussion. The main findings are enough.

It is also useful if the scribes can put down short sayings which mean a lot. For example, some audits I have been involved in recorded:

☐ 'It is lively but not particularly channelled.'
☐ 'They won't volunteer but they are longing to be asked.'
☐ 'Do not create more activity for activity's sake.'

These sort of sayings can often hit home more than loads of good ideas.

Setting up church meetings (for use with methods b or c)
(If Advisers from outside the church are being used they may well guide these meetings.) There will probably be two or more meetings – either weekly or over a weekend. The pattern of the meeting depends on the sort of audit which is being done. Usually it goes something like this:

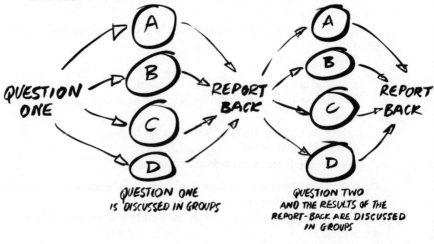

QUESTION ONE
IS DISCUSSED IN GROUPS

QUESTION TWO
AND THE RESULTS OF THE
REPORT-BACK ARE DISCUSSED
IN GROUPS

Things to be arranged:

1 Questions should be given to everyone (or put up where all can see).
2 A stats sheet should be given to everybody.
3 There should be sufficient chairs and enough space for each of the groups to meet without being able to overhear what others are saying.
4 Large sheets of paper or an overhead projector (OHP) should be used to put up the results of the discussion. (These should be kept for use during the summing–up: OHP acetates are easier to deal with.)
5 Refreshments should be available, but kept under control, so that not too much time is spent drinking tea.
6 If you are meeting in a hall, use banners and posters to remind people that this is something which involves God. Start with a *short* period of worship.

Try to get everything arranged well in advance. The atmosphere should be businesslike but friendly.

Getting things over

It is at this time in the audit that communication becomes so important.

When things are communicated there is always a

Sender 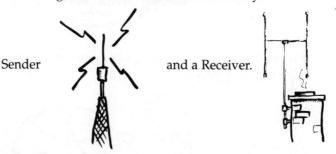 and a Receiver.

There are some things which are worth remembering about getting information from one person to another:

Most obvious but often forgotten: **the receiver is more important than the sender.** The sender may be ever so clever, but if the receiver does not understand then there is **no communication.** (This means that the person in the pew is more important than the preacher!)

Things don't register with the receiver if the sender

- has had a different experience from the receiver. (Try explaining what 'Eastenders ' is all about to someone who has never seen it!)

- is in surroundings which do not match the message. (You can't preach the gospel of love if you are a slavedriver.)

- is not trusted by the receiver. I am sure second-hand car salesmen are very nice people but...

● uses words which do not mean much to the receiver.

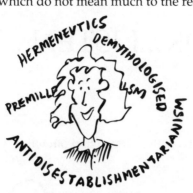

● tries to get too much over at one go.

Whatever you are doing make sure that your communication is communicating.

Having chosen an audit and done the preparation – you need to do it! But, as we've seen, it can be all too easy to look and not see , to listen and not hear. *How* we do an audit – how we look and listen – is vital. More of that in the next chapter!

Chapter 5

LOOK...LISTEN...THINK

Audit begins with trying to find out where you are.

There is more to looking, listening and thinking than you might realise.

To look at something is one thing,

to see what you are looking at is yet another,

to understand what you are seeing is further still,

and to act on your understanding is the highest grace.

Looking at organisations and the people inside them

People see differently although they are looking at the same thing:

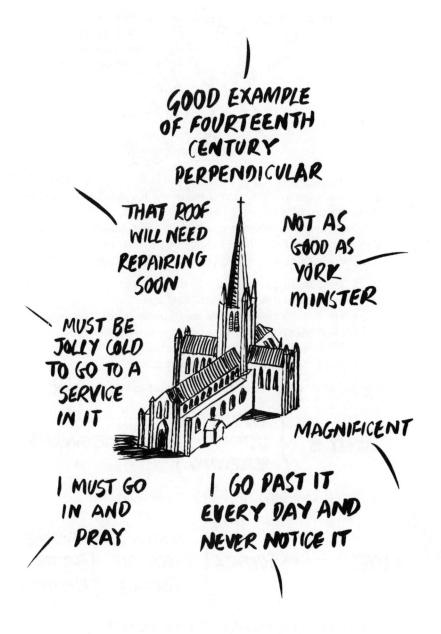

To look well needs *effort* and *knowledge*:

Mrs X has to make the effort to *look carefully* at the tin and has to have the knowledge to *realise* that some of the E's may be substances she doesn't want to give to the children!

So an audit means that you look at your church and your community carefully, knowledgeably, prayerfully.

The sort of questions which you will be asking are:

☐ 'How many people come to this service?'
☐ 'What does this organisation achieve?'
☐ 'How many black people are in positions of leadership?'
☐ 'How many women are in positions of leadership?'
☐ 'How realistic are the dreams of this group?'
☐ 'Are church members spiritually static?'

But above all else: **'What does God want to happen here?'**

$$\text{AUDIT} = \begin{cases} \text{LOOKING} \\ \text{LISTENING} \\ \text{PERCEIVING} \end{cases} = \text{UNDERSTANDING}$$

If you are doing an audit pray for 'X-ray eyes'.

LOOK ——▷ SURFACE) EMOTIONS UNDER THE SURFACE) REASONS FOR THE EMOTIONS

Is the reason a real one? (Or is it just an excuse?)

Christ knew how to **look** – and he saw the inward reality.

- He looked at Jerusalem – and saw the horror which was about to come upon the city (Luke 21:5,6). The disciples only saw the surface – the beautiful buildings.
- He saw the crowd, and realised that they were like sheep without a shepherd: the disciples only saw a crowd.

Christ knew how to **listen** – and heard what was *not* spoken.

- He heard the question of James and John – and knew that what they were really saying was, 'We want to be ahead of the others' (Mark 10:35–40).
- He knew the faith that lay beneath the centurion's words (Luke 7:1–10).
- He realised the trickery which lay behind the questions which the 'disciples of the Pharisees' were asking (Matthew 22:15–22).

Example

A lady complained, 'They no longer sing "Amen" at the end of hymns in our church.'

In fact she was deeply disturbed by changes which had taken place in the church. She came from a broken home which made it difficult to accept anything which upset her pattern of life.

The Adviser needed to hear her, but had to realise that her words were coming from her personal needs and were not a general complaint.

An old man complained, 'We have been turned out of the hall so that you can talk about this airy-fairy stuff.' The Adviser noted the remark and found that there were many other old people who were feeling pushed on one side.

What one person says may be very important because it shows what a lot of people are thinking – but it may be nothing more than a personal gripe.

An Adviser needs to get a 'sense of balance' to see what is important.

An Adviser needs to *'filter'* out the important from many confusing ideas.

An Adviser needs to *pray* that he or she can pick out the right things.

One woman said to an Adviser:

> I've been coming to this church for thirty years and nobody has ever taught me how to pray.

That comment showed that the church was spiritually barren and that it needed to go back to basics. The Adviser had to hear what was being said, and realise that it was important.

The wife of an archdeacon from Botswana was asked to look at the youth work in an English diocese. She wrote as her report:

> Why do you stop your young people coming to church?

That was the heart of it – not what was wrong with the young that they did not go to church, but what was wrong with the church which stopped them coming. It was just the sort of question that Jesus so often asked – going right to the centre of the subject. It is often uncomfortable, as when Jesus said 'I will ask you a question...' in Luke 20:3.

How to look and listen to people

Those who are running an audit need to think how best to get to the bottom of things:

Be still
- to look/listen,
- to pray,
- to think,
- to know the truth.

Ask questions...
- Why did she say that?
- Why did they get so upset about that?
- Why did that go so smoothly?
- What did he get so aggressive about?
- What lay behind that remark?
- What makes this group tick?

Above all – **Where is God in all this?**

? THINK ? ? THINK ? ? THINK ? ? THINK ?

(Remember that Christ is 'renewing your mind' to help you to find out what is his will – Romans 12:2.)

One day the vicar of a city-centre church was talking to me about what God wanted it to do. We agreed to go outside the church and just silently watch the crowds going by. It was a lovely May morning, and we sat for ten minutes just looking and praying. At the end we talked. It was clear that the ministry of the church was not to the office workers, as we had expected. It was to be to those we called 'the little brown bundles' who nobody even noticed – the harassed women with too little money to look after themselves . . . the drifters . . . the unemployed.

It is important to keep a record of what you find out. A simple card index is easiest – you can buy them at most stationers – about 8" by 4" is the right size. You will soon find a way of recording which suits you. I find something like this is helpful...

Date...................................... Place...................................
Seen...
....
....
Heard...
....
....
So...
....
....

(If you like playing with them you can put this information in your computer, but beware of the Data Protection Act 1987.)

Special things to look out for

Discontent
Look out for discontent – without it there will be no change. (See chapter 8 for more about this.)

Fantasies

Look out for fantasies. Sometimes people begin to dream in a way which is unhealthy. Fantasy can take over from facts:

- about the *past*. Often people look back and think there was a 'golden age' in the life of the church – when the church was full, the community was prosperous and the minister a saint. 'Fings ain't what they used to be.'
- about the *present*. This is usually pessimistic: 'Things have been going downhill ever since they changed the services.'

    Or it's optimistic: 'Numbers have doubled since this new man came.' Check the facts.

- about the *future*. This means that people are not using holy common sense. This can lead to a 'faith-auction':

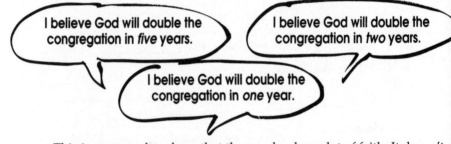

I believe God will double the congregation in *five* years.

I believe God will double the congregation in *two* years.

I believe God will double the congregation in *one* year.

This is supposed to show that the speaker has a lot of faith. It doesn't – but it does show that he or she wants to seem to be a person with a lot of faith.

Hopelessness

Look out for hopelessness. People can sometimes lose all hope. Often nothing has gone right in their own lives, and they think that nothing is possible. If a church has had a long period of decline, a lot of folk may think like this.

An audit will show that change is right and possible. You are saying to the congregation: 'With God "all things are possible" – trust in him, think straight, act sensibly, and he will give you more than you can imagine.' **Do not allow yourself to be dragged down by those who have no hope.**

Happy are those who do what God wants (Matthew 5:6).

Minorities

Look out for minorities. In a congregation there may be all sorts of people who do not have a lot of clout. These may be:

young people	singles	black people
the poor	babies	the 'incomers'

'No change!'

Look out for people who can't cope with change. They may think that **all change is bad**.

Some people find it very difficult to imagine that anything could be different. And because they are rather unsure about themselves they get very upset about anything which is altered.

They want to pull down all those nice houses.

The new minister gives out the notices at the beginning of the service – not like that nice Mr Smith.

Who's moved my vase?

Almost as difficult are those who think that **all change is good**.

These are often rather unsatisfied people, who cannot see what is right in the past, and hope that the future will be better.

I'd scrap the lot.

We can't wait around until all those people have died.

Chuck the junk.

But new is not always good. The Bible talks about both old treasures and new – and the wise man uses both (Matthew 13:52).

Dither

Look out for dither. Some people *do* find it difficult to make decisions. Particularly if someone else has always made up their mind for them. If they have been unemployed for a long time it can get chronic.

Give such people time. Being rushed only makes them upset and unhappy.

But – watch out for people trying to take the easy way out. Sometimes people don't make their mind up because they don't want to take responsibility for what is being decided:

I just want to stand on one side so that I can criticise when things go wrong.

But – watch out for those who are trying to find someone else to make their decisions for them. It is called 'Looking for Daddy' – they want an authority figure to do their thinking for them.

But – watch out for those who are too lazy to think or pray.

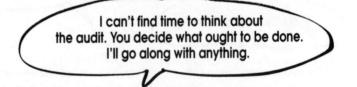

I can't find time to think about the audit. You decide what ought to be done. I'll go along with anything.

An audit tries to help everyone to come to their own decision as to where God is leading the church and what ought to happen. It is not good for them to get out of the pain of making up their mind.

How to look and listen to groups

So far we have thought about what *individuals* say and how they react to things. Now we need to look at the way in which a church congregation reacts.

Groups of people have different outlooks. Your congregation has certain ways of behaving when it is together.

This diagram describes one way of looking at some of these different attitudes. The higher up the diagram you'd mark your

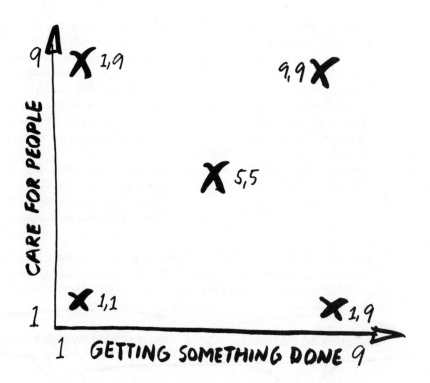

church, the more emphasis is being placed on caring for people. And the further to the right you are, the more emphasis is placed on getting things done. Churches can be in all sorts of places!

Bottom left
This is the 1,1 position. It's easy! This church does not care for people and it isn't getting anything done. It is dead, dead, dead. The resurrecting power of God is its only hope.

Top left
The 1,9 position is much more common. This church cares for people, but doesn't actually do much. It shows in one of two ways:

'Happy Families'

These people think they are just one great big happy family. But they don't really love everybody – just those whose faces fit. They can't put up with someone who upsets them or who is different from them. Years ago a lot of churches like this cold-shouldered people who had just arrived in this country – because their skin was black.

'The Hospital'

Here everyone in the church has come to be made well by the nice doctor in the white coat who is an expert. (This professional is usually the minister.) These people rely on someone else, and so never stand on their own feet. This church runs by trying to clear up the problems of its people. The congregation daren't imagine what life will be like without the expert on whom they all depend so much.

Both sorts of churches are very nice to be part of – as long as nobody starts asking questions. If a new leader (or a mission audit) suggests that God put the church in that area to serve other people he is not very popular.

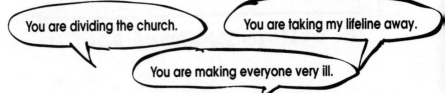

You are dividing the church.

You are taking my lifeline away.

You are making everyone very ill.

But the church is not a mutual admiration society

- it is an army on the march.
- it is some pilgrims on a journey.
- it is a group of servants doing their Master's will.

Bottom right

The 9,1 position is more common than it ought to be. There is a great determination to get something done, but this church doesn't care about people getting hurt in the process.

The attitude (usually of the leaders) is:

We know where we are going. People will just have to come along.

Sometimes it is churchmanship:

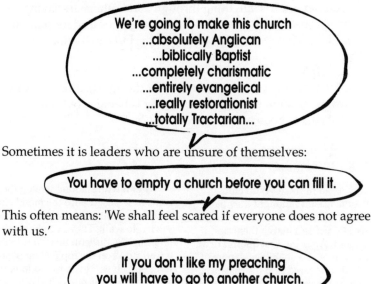

We're going to make this church
...absolutely Anglican
...biblically Baptist
...completely charismatic
...entirely evangelical
...really restorationist
...totally Tractarian...

Sometimes it is leaders who are unsure of themselves:

You have to empty a church before you can fill it.

This often means: 'We shall feel scared if everyone does not agree with us.'

If you don't like my preaching
you will have to go to another church.

This attitude is *horrid*. It shows no love for people and so cannot be a gospel way of behaving. (By the way, if the leadership manages to do what it wants, the church will usually change and become a 1,9 church where everybody is very dependent on the leader.)

In the middle!
What about the 5,5 position? Sometimes it is called the 'middle of the road' position. It looks as though a church like this is both caring for people and getting things done. So it is, but it is not a comfortable church to belong to.

The 'middle of road' is not a safe place to be – ask any hedgehog.

Sometimes this position is called the 'pendulum'. A church will do something (usually have an 'event'). Then it has to stop in order to rush back to look after all the people who are unhappy because nobody is looking after them.

This is particularly difficult for leaders – some people are saying, 'You never carry anything through', and others are saying, 'You never have time to look after me.' And so the poor leaders stand in the middle. They try to please everybody, but satisfy nobody.

Top right
Obviously the church ought to be at the 9,9 position – it is really achieving something and everybody is being cared for.
What is good about the 9,9 position?

Getting there....

Long ago I used to run a youth club.
For some reason I thought they liked to go on long walks. I used to take them into the Peak District and march them up Kinder Scout. After the first quarter of an hour the walk was a shambles – some of them had disappeared into the distance, some of the girls had come in high–heeled shoes and were complaining of blisters. Jack and Jill had disappeared and I was worried about what they were getting up to.
We were in a middle of the road (5,5) position – people were grumbling and we were not getting very much done.

After a while (a long while!) the summit came in sight. At once the mood changed. People forgot their aches and pains and started to walk. They even helped each other up the difficult bits! And in the end we all stood on the top feeling pleased with ourselves. I even found looking after a youth club was not so bad after all.
What had happened? We had moved from a 5,5 to a 9,9 position because they could see the summit. They had a goal to aim for, and everybody wanted to get there.

A church will be in a 9,9 position when it has a goal which everyone has agreed on and which all are trying to achieve.
One of the main jobs of a mission audit is to set the vision – to identify the goal – and help people to accept it.

Chapter 6

DECISION TIME

We are not going to make a plan – nor even use the word. A lot of people have suffered from *planning*: they have seen their homes pulled down, and their families divided and had their benefits cut all because of some plan or other.

Moses did not come down from Mount Sinai with 'the plan' but with the commandments and a vision of the living God.

There are big differences between a vision and a plan.

A vision moves.	A plan can become set in stone.
A vision opens people's eyes.	A plan can care more about itself than people – it tends to move towards a 1,9 position.
A vision helps people to dream dreams.	A plan can make people into robots – just doing what they are told.
A vision is never ending.	A plan has an end.

But if a vision is not 'earthed' it is like a hot air balloon – drifting aimlessly around wherever the wind takes it. It needs to be tied firmly to the real world by a series of *decisions*.

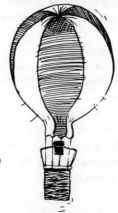

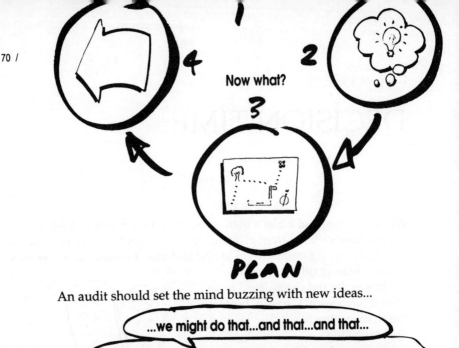

Now what?

PLAN

An audit should set the mind buzzing with new ideas...

...we might do that...and that...and that...

...we have a load more questions we need answers to.

There comes a time when you need to call, 'HALT!'

You can look and think for ever. But there needs to be a cut-off point, when you stop dreaming and start to decide what you must do.

This is a very important time to PRAY. Bring it all to God:

Pray
- for accuracy in finding *his* will among all the ideas and opinions of others.
- for faith to take risks, but the realism of the Holy Spirit not to take the wrong risks.
- for his unity to bind the church together in a time of change.
- for a willingness to accept any necessary pain.

Pin ideas down
Ideas can be like mosquitoes buzzing round and round your head. Catch them by writing them down, or drawing a picture or diagram.

Think of a tree,
The *trunk* is the idea.
The *branches* are the main things to decide if the idea is to happen.
The *twigs* are the details which have to be arranged at the end of each branch.

Example

Trunk: 'Let's have a united witness to the area!'

Branches:

1 A decision to approach other churches to see if they will join in.
2 A decision to mix music/drama/preaching.
3 A decision to use the shopping precinct if possible.
4 A decision to spend £40 on printed material.

Twigs:
Branch 1 means

(a) Peggy is to approach the minister's fraternal and see if they are interested.
(b) John is to talk to the Methodist minister to see if their men's group would come and help.

Branch 2 means

(a) Sue will see how many people in church who play anything can be got together to practise the music.
(b) Harry will see if the youth group can repeat the play they did in church last autumn.

...and so on and so on!

Decision making

First things first
Do the three things in order.

1 **Trunk** – get the main idea clear in everybody's mind.
2 **Branches** – think of the main areas which need to be organised.
3 *then* deal with the **twigs**.

Otherwise people become bogged down with the details and forget the reason for it all. Sometimes people get into difficulties because they fasten on some detail (a twig) far too early. They start to think about it, find it difficult and then throw their hands into the air and say, 'It is beyond us.'

It can help to get a big sheet of paper (flip-chart size or bigger) and draw a *decision diagram*.

Write the central idea (the trunk) in the central circle.
Label each branch.
Put twigs on the end of each branch.

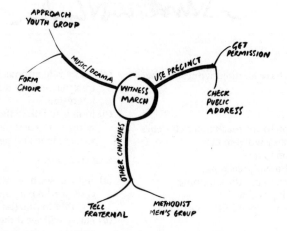

If you do not make your idea clear and set out what needs to be done then you get

confusion . . . frustration . . . upset

...and your bright new idea will just trickle away to nothing.

Pray

Planning and prayer are not two different things. Often people find that as they pray about a project, God shows them a fresh slant on what is being thought of or a new difficulty which needs to be tackled.

Pray during your planning and plan during your prayers.

Involve people

Planning is done by people. This can be:

(a) a group of people chatting together.

(b) brainstorming: where a smallish group of people just throw a lot of ideas around (however silly some of them may seem). Don't stop to discuss them – just get somebody to jot them down so that they are not forgotten. Don't be frightened by a bit of chaos and humour. Only talk about each item in turn when you have run out of steam. This is great for helping people to widen their horizons: often you find that the wildest ideas produce the best results.

(c) one or two people sitting down and then presenting their ideas to a group or committee.

(d) one person saying, 'This is how it is to be done!'

On the whole the best planning is done by a group of people:

● not too many, or it gets confused.
● not too few, or it just becomes 'X's idea'.

Note: Research has shown that people are committed to carrying out a project if they are deeply involved in the planning.

Beware of 'risky-shift'! This can happen when a group of people start thinking together – they will tend to suggest more risky ideas than if they were making the decision by themselves. This may be because they are not going to be held personally responsible for what is decided. Or it can be that they get faith from what other people say.

Watch out!

Beware of 'committeeitis'. Planning groups should not become committees. Watch out for committees where:

● one or two people do the work and the rest criticise.
● people get too formal. It can happen that outside the meeting room people say, 'Hello Jack', 'Hello Jane', but during the committee meeting they call each other 'Mr Smith'...'Mrs Jones'.
● it is dominated by those who can talk fast — sensible, slower folk who have much to give get squashed.
● prayer can evaporate, and the atmosphere of the Sunday service is totally different from that of the meeting on the following evening.

Nevertheless many churches have committees. It can be said:
A committee works best when it stops acting like a committee and becomes a group of Christian friends trying to extend the Kingdom of God together.

However, nearly all of us have to work with committees at some point. If you are on a committee, remember that the tree is important here as well.

Decisions, decisions!

Each decision has five parts:

What exactly is being decided?

Everybody needs to be clear in their own minds what exactly is being decided. This is the 'branch'. It is too easy to make a quick decision because not all those present know what is being arranged.

It helps if the secretary writes it down – often trying to put it on paper makes people realise what is happening. A committee can spend ten minutes discussion in making a decision. Then they ask the secretary to read it out – and then they spend two hours *really* coming to the decision!

The various 'twig' decisions on details follow.

Who is going to carry it out?

This needs to be clear. Many committees make great decisions, but nobody carries them out – so they are a waste of time. In any big decision there may be a whole team of people involved – each playing a part – and the committee needs to ensure that everybody knows what to do and when to do it.

'Too many decisions are like tired old men: they totter out for a while, and then go home and fall asleep'.

If it is a big job it also needs to be decided if the people doing it are to report back from time to time, to tell the committee what is happening.

When will it be finished?

Things can drag on and on like a ten foot snake. It is important to set a date by which the project should have *started* and a date by which it should be *finished*.

Who else needs to know?
One Church Committee decided that there were too many pews in the church and not enough space for people to gather after the services. So they decided to take out the back three pews and carpet the area. But they did not tell anyone else except the builder who was to do the work. Not suprisingly the congregation were upset: 'Our church is being turned upside down and nobody told us anything about it.'

Make sure that as many people as possible know about the decision. It is sensible and polite to do so.

The committee needs to decide how this communication is to take place: is it to be a notice given out in church, something pinned to the noticeboard, an article in the newsheet – or what?

Who is going to check on progress?
Somebody needs to be in charge of each project decided upon. (This person is a 'progress-chaser'.) This is particularly true if outsiders are being used: eg builders, a mission team from another church, an outside speaker.

Every committee needs to check frequently that each decision which it has made is being carried out.

The end
It is not too early to start deciding what you are going to do once the audit is over.

Why not have a 'prayer party' – where you begin the evening by everybody bringing some food to share with others. Start with a time of thanksgiving to God for the time of discovery together, followed by a really good meal together and some games or whatever else folk would like to do.

In the north–west of England a shared meal is called 'Jacob's joint'. Nobody seems to know why!

Chapter 7

GETTING IT DONE

There is more to doing something than just deciding on the vision and then working out the branches and the twigs.

We all know it is easier to decide to do something than actually to do it – particularly if we are not too keen on doing it in the first place! I have lots of paint brushes but they do not get used very much. I often decide I am going to start decorating – tomorrow!

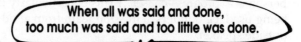

**When all was said and done,
too much was said and too little was done.**

The Christian leader has to help people to begin to put what has been decided into action...and then make sure that it gets finished.

Take our decision diagram on page 71. If Peggy forgets to talk to the minister's fraternal and Harry can't be bothered to get round to mentioning the drama to the youth group, then those who have done their job will feel let down. The mission may be a flop, or not even take place, and the name of Jesus Christ will be injured by shoddy workmanship.

The church is full of bones:

● wish–bones – who wish someone else would do the work,
● jaw–bones – who talk a lot but do little else,
● knuckle–bones – who knock what everyone else does,
● back–bones – who get down and actually do the work.
(William Wilkerson)

How can Christians help each other to keep up to the mark? There are some golden rules.

Rule 1

Keep praising! Yes, keep praising God, but keep praising each other too. A thimbleful of thanks is better than a bucketful of blame. If people have not done much with their lives, they will have a very low picture of themselves and think they cannot do anything worthwhile. If they are praised for something, however small, it will help them to grow as people because they will know that someone else thinks that they are valuable. Such people **expect to fail**, so anything which they think is criticism will make them curl up inside.

In particular one of the most important steps anyone can take as a Christian is to know that God has used **them** – not the minister or that mature Christian they have always looked up to – but them. When this happens they need to be assured that this is so by a Christian leader.

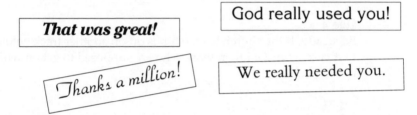

That was great!

God really used you!

Thanks a million!

We really needed you.

Rule 2

Keep up the team spirit. Most people in the inner–cities are used to working together with others. They may be less used to working by themselves without anyone looking over their shoulder. See the church as a football team, where each is dependent on everyone else – and if the goalie has gone off home for tea the whole team suffers. (St Paul did not use the picture of a football team – in 1 Corinthians 12 he used the picture of a body – but the idea is the same.)

The feeling of being part of a team can be helped by continually explaining where each bit of work fits into the whole. People don't mind being cogs if they can get a picture of the whole machine.

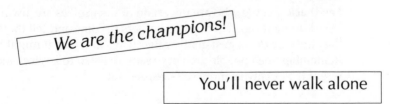

We are the champions!

You'll never walk alone

Rule 3

Set a high standard. If a Christian leader is sloppy in his or her own work, careless in valuing people and lacking in prayer, then others will copy faithfully!

But be careful: some leaders expect everyone else to come up to their own high standards, and are hurt when they do not. They need to be prepared for someone to produce only second-rate work – it may be the first time that the person has ever done anything which is not third-rate!

Rule 4

Be steady. If the church leadership is off on another track before the first task is finished then those who are supposed to get on with it will feel left behind.

> Erratic people seldom make good leaders because they leave uncertainty and confusion in their wake.

Rule 5

Feedback. People who are uncertain of themselves are always asking, 'Am I doing it right?' They need others to come and tell them that they are – or to suggest gently other ways in which it might be done. Remember such people are very ready to listen to advice, and do not resent it as easily as more self–assured folk.

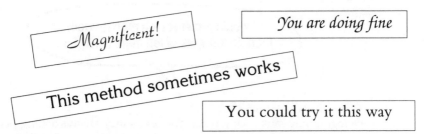

Magnificent!

You are doing fine

This method sometimes works

You could try it this way

Rule 6

Remember every person is a human being. Each person who is doing something to make sure that each objective of the church is reached is a human being with needs and hopes and only a certain amount of time. With good leadership, people in the inner–cities will do a very great deal, but this must not be taken advantage of. Their home life should not suffer, their own leisure time has to be remembered, and they must find Christ in what they are doing. Leaders need to take particular care of those who are working hard for the cause of Christ and his church.

On the other hand it must be remembered that many people have found an enormous happiness in working in this way, and have grown greatly in the process. A great remark to hear is:

> **If you had told me last year that I'd be doing this now......**

Those who are unemployed feel as though they have been thrown on the rubbish dump – they can regain their self–respect by working with the church. They can be made to feel real people again. One man said, 'When I was made redundant it was as though I had turned into a piece of glass – people just looked right through me.' Encourage them to join the church team.

Handing things on

All Christian leaders need to give other people things to do: to delegate. It can be asking someone to become a Sunday school teacher, lead a house group, be in charge of repainting the hall etc, etc.

But it is not always easy to do it:

1 because we do not know who to ask,
2 because we are unsure of what we want,
3 because we do not know how to train them.

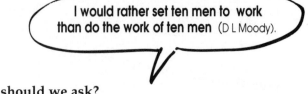

I would rather set ten men to work
than do the work of ten men (D L Moody).

Who should we ask?

Delegation means taking risks. You are nearly always asking people to do something they have never done before – therefore neither you nor they know if they will be able to do it.

Asking someone to do a job nearly always means giving them responsibility. In some deprived areas not too many people have had the chance of personal responsibility, so you are giving that person a real opportunity for growing spiritually and as a human being. They need all the encouragement you can give them.

LOOK INTO THE BIBLE
Luke 6:12–16

Note:

1 Choosing people is such an important part of leadership that we need to take time off to get right away from the ordinary pressures of life – 'into the hills'.

2 Be prepared to take time praying – Jesus 'spent the night praying to God'. Often leaders find that, as they pray, someone in the congregation floats into their mind and they say, 'Why did I not think of X before?'

3 While leaders will take advice from other people, the choice has got to be theirs – 'He called...chose...designated.'

4 Jesus did not choose the obvious people. They were a very mixed bunch of people – different backgrounds, education, social class, political views. They did not get on easily with each other.

5 We know from the rest of the Gospels that they caused him much disappointment and heartache.

6 One of them let him down competely – Judas 'became a traitor'.

7 But they were the ones whom God wanted – even Judas.

Very often the right people are not the obvious ones. A school teacher is not always right to teach in Sunday school, or someone who works in a bank to be treasurer. It can be that the 'little ones', who have never been able to do much with their life, will give more prayer, more care and more time than others who seem to have more qualifications. But they will need a lot of support, especially in the early days.

What should we ask them to do?

This seems a silly question. But if we are not clear what is involved in being a Sunday school teacher or in leading the youth group then we shall not be able to ask them properly.

We need to know:

- what skills the job demands,
- how much training we can offer them,
- how much time the work involves,
- whether there are any breaks for holidays etc,
- who they have to work with – and who is in charge!
- how much money they can spend,
- how long we expect the job to last,
- whether or not we shall be able to support them closely,
- ....and – above all – what the church expects to happen.

If we cannot set an objective in front of people we are only asking them to fill a gap, not do a job.

It is only when we have got answers to these questions in our head that we should go and ask someone to do the job.

When you see the person:

- remember that you are putting a lot of information in front of them. They will need to have it repeated several times before they can take it all in.
- don't ask for an answer on the spot – even if they say, 'Yes.' Give them time so that they can work it through and take a well–thought out and prayerful decision.
- talk through what they may need to drop in order to make space for the new job.
- give them time to ask lots of questions.

How can we train them?

It is useful to think of how the person may have been trained in the past. If they have been to college then a course of lectures and written work may be right.

But most people have not been to college and these methods merely make them feel inadequate.

Jesus trained the seventy–two 'others' in Luke 10 by:

1 having them around him while he did the job,
2 sending them out to do what he had done – 'preach...heal',
3 making sure they reported back to him,
4 correcting them if necessary.

This 'on the job' training is best for nearly everybody. Imagine a craftsman on a lathe teaching an apprentice. He shows him how to do it many times, and then he says, 'You have a go.' He patiently watches and corrects until it is right.

That is how new teachers and leaders in the Kingdom can be helped – to watch a good example, learn from others, and then to do it – with lots of opportunities to discuss what they are doing.

Seek first the Kingdom

Christian leaders are not always good at delegating. Often they are very hard–working and thorough people themselves and they need to make sure that they do not hug everything to themselves.

If you are a Christian leader and are thinking like this, then you need to pick up your Bible and take a good dose of the ministry of Jesus. You will find he was remarkably unfussed by other people's mistakes, squabbles and silliness. He was the original 'laid back' man. He was often let down, often drawn into the small–minded tiffs of the disciples and in the end 'they all forsook him and fled.' **But he went on believing in them.**

Chapter 8

ALL CHANGE!

Mission audit means *making things change* – so that:

- good things in the church become better,
- useless things are weeded out,
- new ideas are brought in sensibly.

But change is difficult for people to accept – and we need to think why this is so. And remember:

- during change we need to *care* for the people who are being upset by the change.
- change must make the *vision* clearer.
- There are certain simple rules about change which a leader needs to know.

Rule 1

People will not want change if they are happy with things as they are. It's obvious when you think about it. If people see no need to change they won't want to! Only when people are unhappy with the present are they prepared to face change in the future.

One church had only sixteen members left. One person spoke for them all: 'We are not as many as we used to be, but we have always been a very happy family church; we don't need to alter anything.' None of them was less than sixty–five years old.

I like my old pullovers: my wife says they are a disgrace. 'Why change?' say I. I will only change when I realise that the old one has fallen to pieces. In other words, I am only prepared to change when I am fed up with the present situation.

LOOK INTO THE BIBLE

Jesus said: 'I have not come to call the righteous, but sinners to repentance' (Luke 5:32). Is it possible to repent without being prepared to change? The 'righteous' have the 'I'm all right, Jack' attitude that does not want to be disturbed by Jesus.

Who is closer to God – the righteous?...or the sinner?

What does this say to a church?

A diagram will show what happens:

The bottom line shows the 'level of discontent' – the further along from zero you go the greater the unhappiness in the church. The vertical line marks the 'possibility of change'. It shows how much change is possible without too many difficulties.

The line like a hoop shows how easy or difficult it will be to change things – depending on how content, or otherwise, people are with things now.

So when the line is at the bottom left there is no unhappiness in the church and therefore no possibility of change: 'We are all very happy – leave us alone.' At the top of the 'hoop' there is the greatest possibility of change. Discontent is fairly high – though not at its greatest. This is the point where most people are saying, 'We have got to do something about it' – and rather looking forward to getting it done.

But note that if the change is not made at this top point then the line moves over to the going down side. Discontent gets worse, but now people are frustrated and rebellious because nothing has happened. Now they tend to say, 'What's the use?' if changes are suggested.

Example

In 1977 the management of a ball-bearing factory introduced the idea that new production methods should be brought in 'to save labour costs'. Not surprisingly the workforce objected because they saw their jobs at risk. They took strike action and the plan was dropped. By the early 1980s it was clear to everyone that imports were taking over the market and it was difficult to sell the ball bearings made at the factory because they were too expensive. There were many redundancies. It was not until 1986 that the new production methods were brought in – but by that time the workforce were unhappy, frustrated and rebellious. 'Should have been done years ago!' was the cry. The new practices were objected to and only accepted with much bad feeling.

Perhaps the managers should have spelt out the real reason for slimming down in 1977 – that the order books were declining. When people were ready for change in the early '80s the new ways should have been introduced. By 1986 they were well over the hill and the few workpeople who were left were depressed and accustomed to failure.

Before introducing any proposal to deal with a problem, make sure that everyone knows that there is something wrong!

It is not enough for only one or two people to be aware that there is a problem to solve – spend time spelling out exactly what it is to everyone who needs to know. Only then will they be prepared to listen to an answer.

Rule 2

If you want to introduce change, do your cockpit drill.

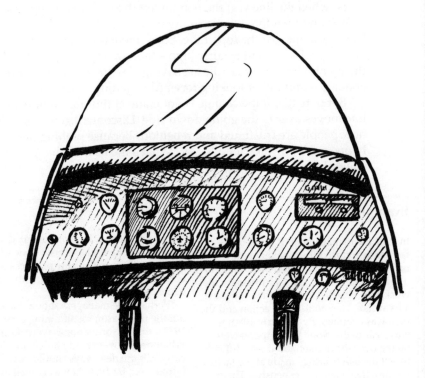

Every pilot needs information – and has meters to provide it.

 **Artificial horizon:** this shows the attitude of the plane – whether it is climbing, turning, diving.

During a time of change, keep things as steady as possible. Don't make unnecessary changes. What change *really* needs to happen?

Airspeed indicator: this shows how fast the plane is going through

the air.

Change things too quickly and people will be confused and upset. Change too slowly and people will not notice that anything is happening and so will stay discontented.

Altimeter: this shows how high the plane is.

People are frightened by heights. How much fear is there in the church? Are a lot of people getting white–knuckled?

Rate of climb indicator: this shows how fast the plane is climbing

or diving.

How *much* change is happening? Is there just a small change or an about turn? (Some churches loop the loop and wonder why people feel sick.)

Fuel gauge: this shows how much fuel (power) is left.

How strong is the desire for change in the church? If a lot of people want change very much it puts a great deal more steam behind the change than a few people vaguely wishing that something would happen.

If leaders want to introduce change sensibly they need to do their cockpit drill. Remember that it is not the amount of fear etc that the leader feels which matters, but how much is felt by the bulk of the congregation. At this stage leaders often misread their congregation. A leader who says, 'We shouldn't do that or everyone will be upset', may mean, 'I am feeling scared.'

Rule 3

People will be more ready to accept change if they *trust* the pilot!
A leader who is trusted by people will be able to bring in change much more easily than someone who is looked upon with suspicion.

Leaders need to make sure that the reasons they are introducing a change are truly Christian. Is it

- to boost yourself, and show how effective you are?
- to make people do what you want?
- to get your opinion accepted?

Or is it to show Christ's love to people and the church through the change?

What is trust?

It is being –

Thoroughly

Reliable

Under

Severe

Testing

It is interesting to think of what we look for in those we trust – a doctor, a minister or a lawyer. It probably means things like:

☐ dependability   ☐ sincerity   ☐ skill at their job

☐ human warmth   ☐ integrity   ☐ sensitivity

and so on....

LOOK INTO THE BIBLE

'If one of you wants to be great, he must be the servant of the rest; and if one of you wants to be first, he must be the slave of all. For even the Son of Man did not come to be served; he came to serve and to give his life to redeem many people' (Mark 10:43–45).

A Christian leader is a 'servant of the servants of the Servant.'

How far was Christ prepared to go to serve us?

Rule 4

Tell people the reasons for the change in a way they can understand.
Remember:

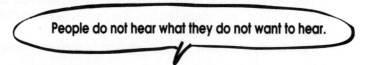

People do not hear what they do not want to hear.

Some find talking of change makes them uneasy, so they find it difficult to hear what is being said.

It is not enough to give out a notice in church or write an article in the parish magazine – people will not understand it. They will become nervous, and probably misunderstand what is being suggested.

People have to be told
...in several different ways
...over a fair period of time
...in language they can understand.

Tell....
- by talking with people one to one.
- by preaching sermons.
- by magazines...local media.
- by special letters to individuals.

Show
- Take people to see a good example of a church where the change has already taken place.
- Get people who have been through the change to come and say what they feel about it.
- Put up posters etc.
- Use diagrams, pictures and maps wherever possible.

Notices don't work
A vicar gave out a notice that there would be no evening service in the parish church the following Sunday because they were joining with the Methodists for their service. Despite this nearly half the congregation who heard the notice still turned up at the parish church. 'Why did nobody tell us?' they said!

Rule 5

Try to understand why people are objecting to the change, and how you can help them.

Sometimes a leader who introduces change will come up against a brick wall. *Don't* just shout louder...it only makes the wall higher. Find out why there is a wall there.

People oppose a new idea for all sorts of reasons, mainly because

- they are frightened, or
- they don't understand what it's all about, or
- they feel their own position threatened,

or sometimes all three at once.

If someone is against the idea you have put forward – try to find out the reason. (Do it privately. Don't do it in a group – nobody likes climbing down in public.)

Rule 6

Don't have it all cut and dried.

People like to be people not rubber stamps.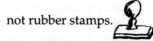

Involve people as early as possible, and do not present a package which cannot be changed.

Be prepared to try something out for an experimental period. This shows that your own mind is not completely made up, and that you are prepared to listen to what other people are saying.

There are several stages in getting a group of people to accept change:

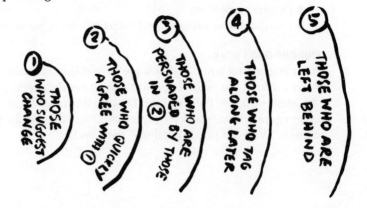

Note: the people who are best at persuading others that a change is right are *not* the people who first thought of it. They are too enthusiastic and too sold on the idea. The most persuasive are those in group 2 – the first to be persuaded.

So, if you are introducing an idea, persuade a few people. Then sit back and let *them* get on with convincing the others.

Example

At a Church Committee meeting the minister suggested a change in the time of the morning service, and set out his reasons. Several people said, 'Why change?' He saw the question as a personal attack on himself and began to get angry. The meeting ended with no decision being made. The minister was disheartened and the rest were confused.

He could have:

1 spelt out the problem to be solved.

2 put forward the change of time of service as a possible answer.

3 kept quiet and let those who agreed with him persuade the others.

4 suggested it should be tried for an experimental period.

Rule 7

Have courage!

The leader who suggests change is seldom popular! Don't worry! Leaders are not given the job in order to be popular but to make things happen.

Dangers for leaders!
1 Withdrawing from the battle and letting it all happen around you. People will get confused because there is no leadership.
2 Being inflexible and unwilling to listen to the opinions of others.
3 Losing the vision. It is easy when arguing about the details of a change to forget why you proposed it in the first place.
4 Being too intense about it. Introduce a new idea casually so that other people do not get put on the defensive.
5 Getting angry with those who disagree with you. If you lose your temper it will make it more difficult for everyone.

Leaders have to create tomorrow.

LOOK INTO THE BIBLE

Read Joshua 1:1–9. How are these instructions for leaders' based on this passage?
  (a) Do not compare yourself with the person who had the job before you.
  (b) God has chosen you for a particular job.
  (c) Stay close to God.
  (d) Remember God's promises.
  (e) Be brave!
  (f) Depend on God, not people.

Learn by heart: 'I will never leave you nor forsake you.'

THE FAITH CIRCLE

There are two kinds of faith.
  Imagine that your faith is like a circle. Inside the circle is **settled faith**.

Inside that circle you do your Christian thing – all those things you feel comfortable with. For example, you may feel comfortable going to church... praying...reading the Bible. Put a cross for everything you feel comfortable doing as a Christian. (Notice that while you may feel happy doing these things – others may not.) Your faith circle is not the same as someone else's.

But God does not leave us happily in our 'settled faith' circle. He is very liable to call us to do something which is outside the circle – and outside there is *fear*.
  Think of all the people in the Bible who were called to step outside their 'settled faith' to do something they were uncomfortable with.

- Abraham – 'Leave your country' (Genesis 12:1–5).
- Moses – 'I am sending you to Pharaoh' (Exodus 3:1– 4:17).
- Jeremiah – 'I appointed you a prophet' (Jeremiah 1:4–19).
- Jonah – 'Go to the great city of Nineveh' (Jonah 1:1–3).
- The seventy–two – 'Go! I am sending you' (Luke 10:1–9).
- Ananias – 'Go to the house on Straight Street' (Acts 9:1–19).

How many others can you think of? Can you think of *any* followers of God in the Bible who were *not* asked to step outside their 'settled faith' circle?

As you look at the Bible passages listed above you will notice that people often *argued* with God. They made all sorts of excuses why they should not do what he wanted. We do this because we are moving into the place of fear – and so we try to wriggle out of it.

We can:

- say, 'No!' to God – and disobey him completely.
- put it off – and hope it will go away. (Sometimes Christians are trying to put it off when they say, 'I'll pray about it': it sounds better!)
- do something else – being busy keeps us from finding out what God really wants us to do.
- think of all the possible difficulties – until the idea is drowned in the cold water. (One way of dealing with this is to look carefully at each difficulty in turn and answer it.)
- look for someone else to tell us what to do.

You get out of the circle by simply *obeying* God. You may feel fearful, but it does not matter what you feel. When you step over the circle you are entering what we will call **pilgrim faith.**

Paul describes how he came to preach in Corinth 'in weakness and fear' (1 Corinthians 2:3). If Paul was allowed to feel like that, so are we.

'Pilgrim faith'

● is faith which is going somewhere,
● is obedient faith,
● is faith on the move.

We need both 'settled faith' and 'pilgrim faith'.
'Settled faith' gives us a stable background of Christian faith and behaviour.
'Pilgrim faith' keeps us on our toes, helps us to grow, and makes us humble before God.

All this matters when you are leading a *group* of people in a change. A group also has its faith circle.

A committee may feel safe discussing buildings or finance...but it may not feel safe talking about evangelism or the spiritual temperature of the church.

A Bible study group may feel safe discussing the book of Hosea...but it may not feel safe when talking about how they can put the teachings of the book into practice.

A group of people react in just the same way as a single person when they are faced with fear...They may

● refuse to do God's will.
● put it off ('to a future meeting').
● do something else ('pass to the next item on the agenda').
● pour cold water on the proposal for change.
● look for authority ('the last minister never did that sort of thing').

But when a group does obey God and accept change it finds great joy – like the seventy–two in Luke 10 they come back 'with joy' and make their Lord 'full of joy through the Holy Spirit'. The rule is:

When God asks you to do something – do it!

CONCLUSION

So, you've made it to the end of the book! I hope you've discovered the excitement of mission audit – and begun to grapple with looking at your church, listening to God and acting on what you've found out. To do that is risky, unnerving – frightening, even. But stepping, as a church, into 'pilgrim faith' is what it's all about: a journey of discovery into what it means to be God's people, God's church.

'...to him be glory in the church...'

APPENDIX

A Stats sheet

Local facts need to be set out for all to see.

Put on a sheet of paper the facts you can find out:

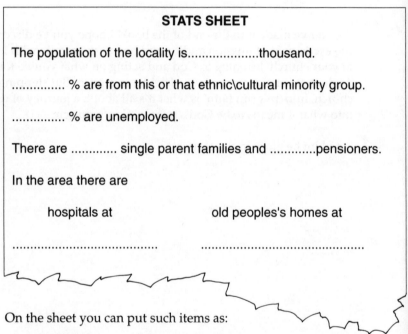

STATS SHEET

The population of the locality is...................thousand.

.... % are from this or that ethnic\cultural minority group.

.... % are unemployed.

There are .... single parent families and ....pensioners.

In the area there are

hospitals at   old peoples's homes at

....

On the sheet you can put such items as:

- schools
- other churches (and their approximate size of congregation),
- non-Christian places of worship,
- the places where people meet,
- the crime figures....

– anything which you feel might help the people in the group to learn about their area and be able to talk sense.